Harry Potter
SPIROGLYPHICS®

Thunder Bay Press
An imprint of Printers Row Publishing Group
10350 Barnes Canyon Road, Suite 100, San Diego, CA 92121
www.thunderbaybooks.com • mail@thunderbaybooks.com

Copyright © 2021 Warner Bros. Entertainment Inc.
WIZARDING WORLD characters, names, and related
indicia are © & ™ Warner Bros. Entertainment Inc.
WB SHIELD: © & ™ WBEI. Publishing Rights © JKR. (s21)

Printers Row Publishing Group is a division of Readerlink Distribution Services, LLC. Thunder Bay Press is a registered trademark of Readerlink Distribution Services, LLC.

Correspondence regarding the content of this book should be sent to Thunder Bay Press, Editorial Department, at the above address.

Thunder Bay Press
Publisher: Peter Norton
Associate Publisher: Ana Parker
Art Director: Charles McStravick
Senior Developmental Editor: April Graham Farr
Developmental Editor: Diane Cain
Editor: Jessica Matteson
Production Team: Rusty von Dyl, Beno Chan, Mimi Oey

ISBN: 978-1-64517-291-8

Printed in Malaysia

25 24 23 22 21   1 2 3 4 5

Harry Potter

SPIROGLYPHICS®

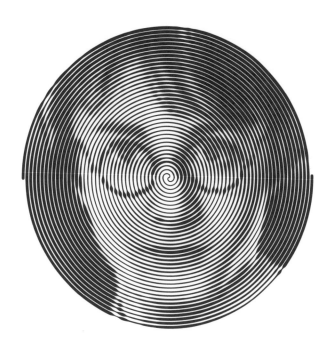

BEST–SELLING
AUTHOR

THOMAS
PAVITTE

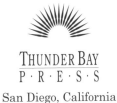

THUNDER BAY
P·R·E·S·S

San Diego, California

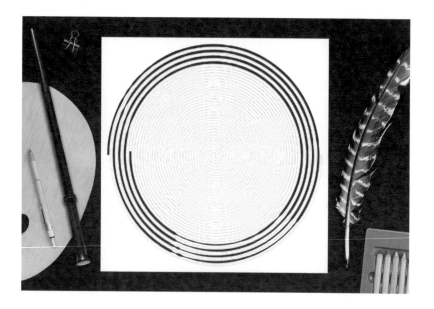

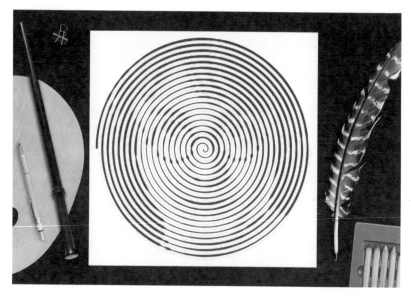

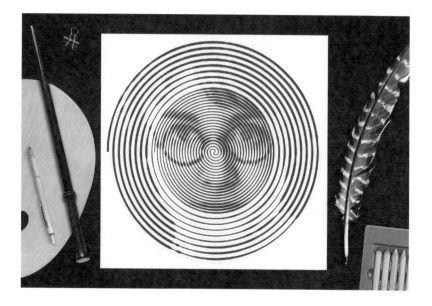

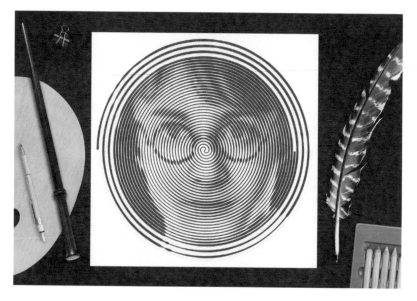

MAGICALLY CREATE HARRY POTTER WORKS OF ART

At first glance, spiroglyphics appear to be nothing but simple spirals. If you look a little closer, you'll see that the lines are two spirals, joined at the middle, subtly varying in width as they wind to the center. When you pick up a pen and begin to fill in the lines, like magic from your wand, a character or creature from the Harry Potter films begins to emerge!

INSTRUCTIONS

To create an element of surprise, pick any puzzle to begin. Or, you can refer to the key in the back of the book and choose your puzzle. It's up to you how you approach it!

Choose one of the enclosed-loop ends on the outside of the spiral—the one on the left side of the puzzle or the right side of the puzzle—to begin. You can start on either side. Use your favorite marker or pen to fill in the lines and work your way around the spiral. When you reach the center of the spiral, stand back and take a look. Can you tell what it is yet? Then, work your way back from the center to the outside and you'll see more details appear! As you stand back from the image, the character or creature comes into focus. Spiroglyphics are fun for wizards and Muggles alike!

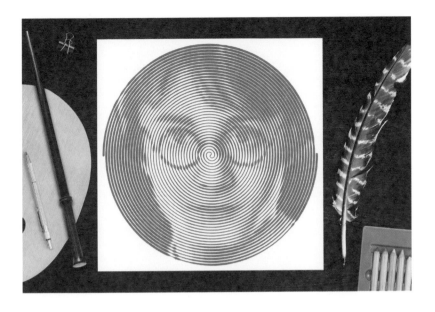

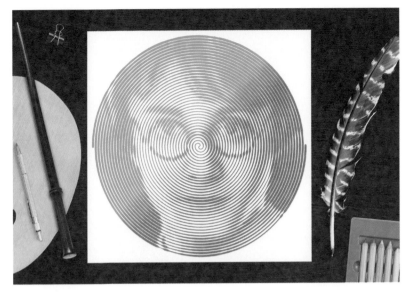

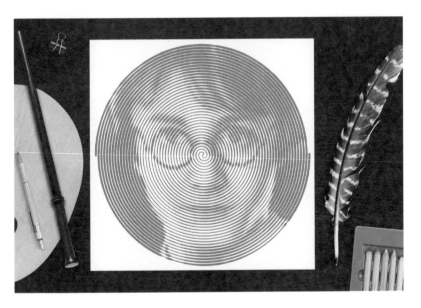

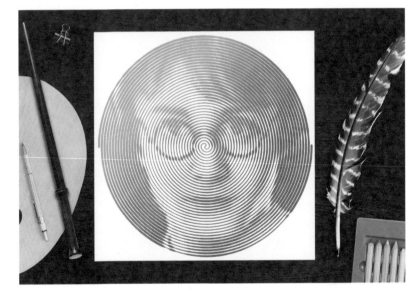

TRY THESE TECHNIQUES

The simplest way to create the spiroglyphics is with a black felt-tip pen for a monochromatic look, but there are endless variations you can try to achieve fun effects.

- After you've completed the image, go back and color in the white background spiral too. Try different color combinations, like contrasting colors or light and dark shades of the same color.

- Use realistic colors for a pop-art look. Give Mad-Eye Moody his electric-blue false eye or Fawkes his vibrant red and gold plumage.

- Divide the spiroglyphic into sections and use a different color for each part. You can split the puzzle in half or get creative with different shapes.

- Choose a number of rings to complete in one color then switch to another color to give your spiroglyphic a gradient effect.

START YOUR COLLECTION

Once you've finished a puzzle, carefully tear it out at the perforation line. Tweet, share, and frame your *Harry Potter Spiroglyphics* masterpiece!

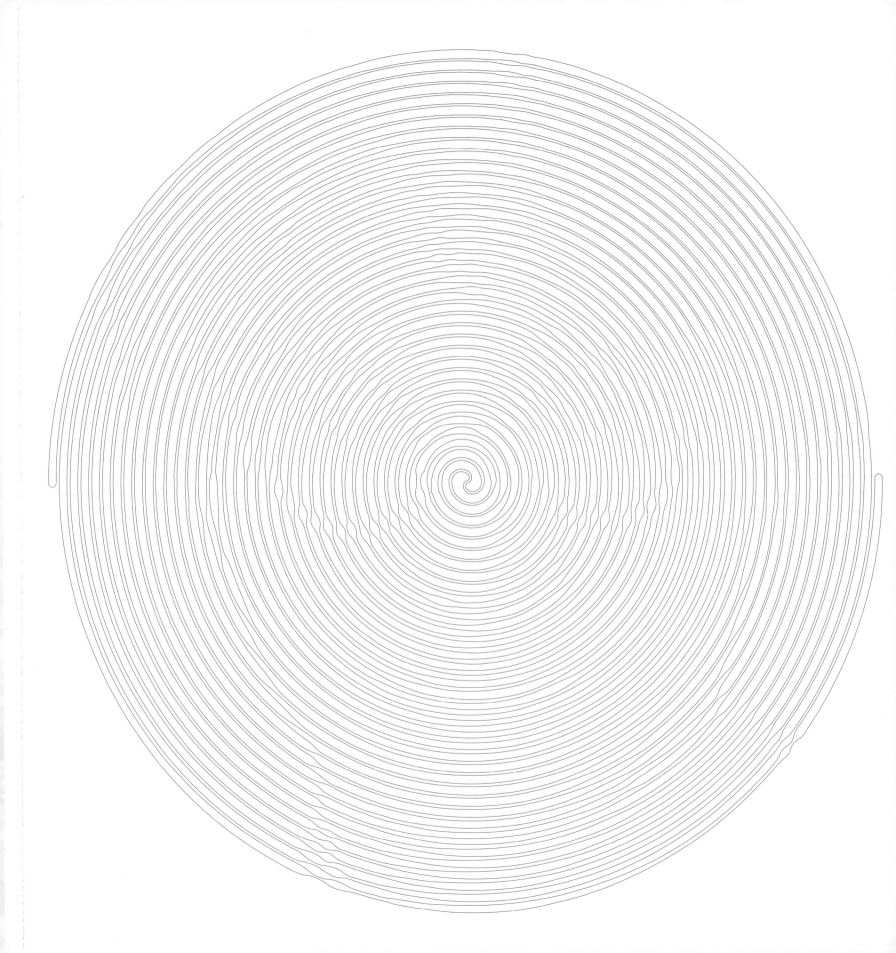

4>

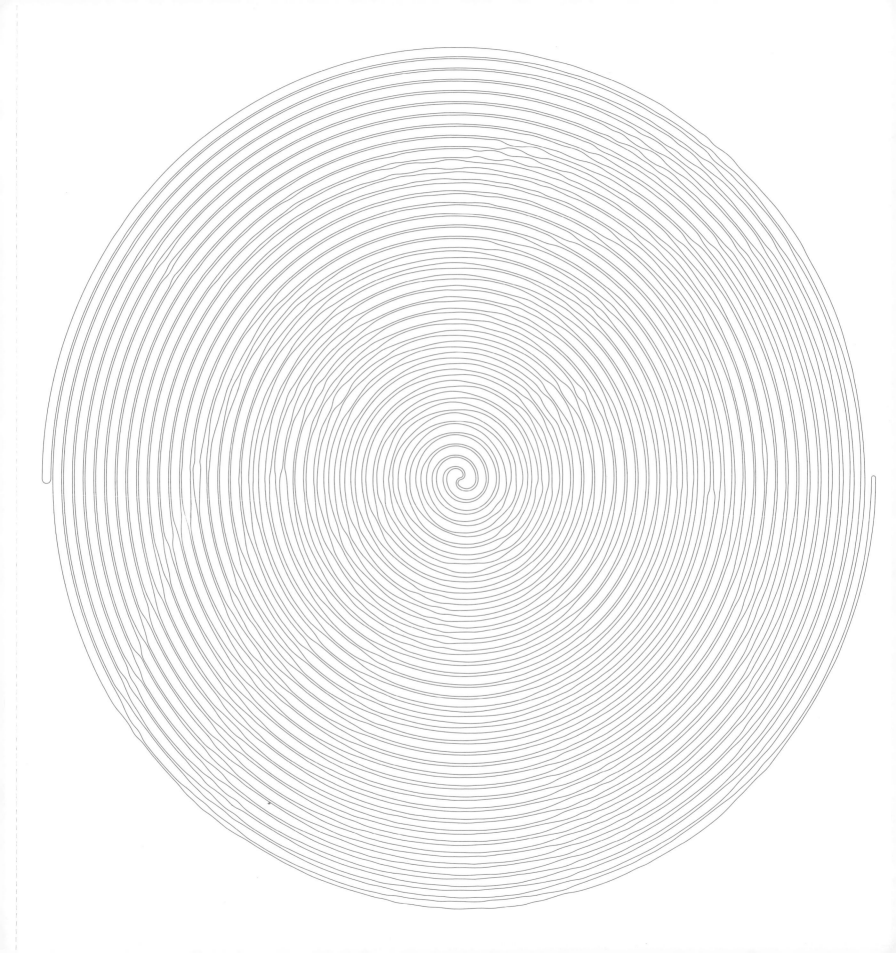

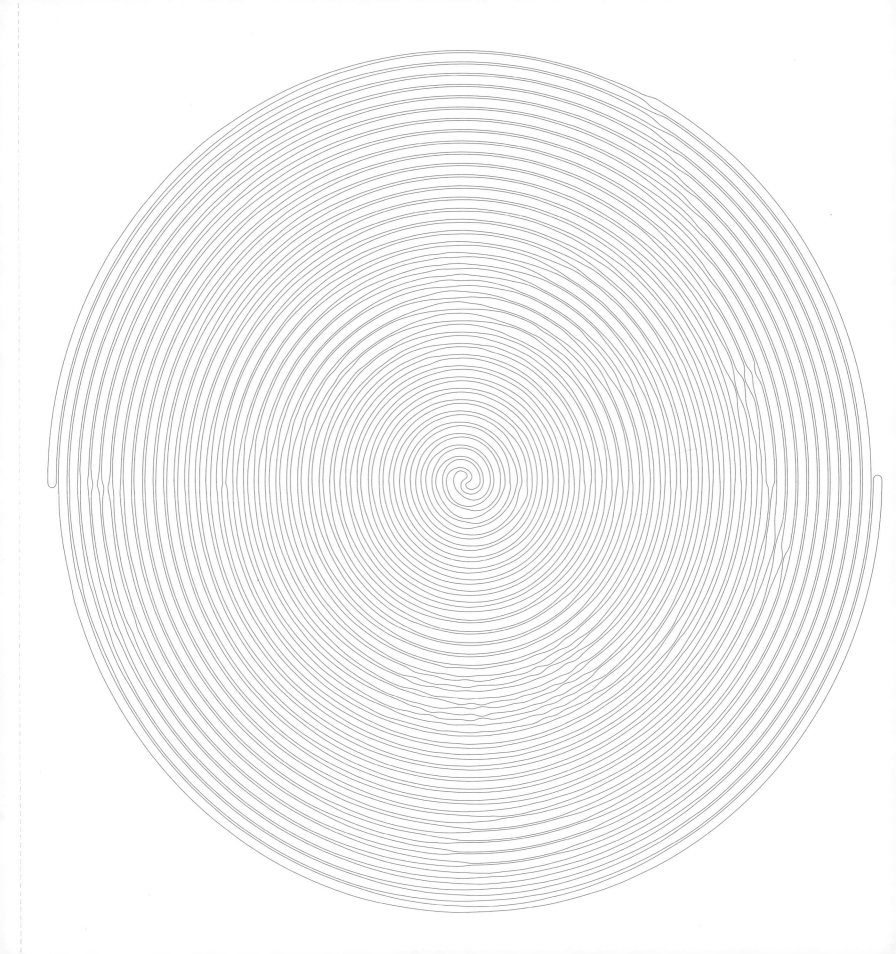

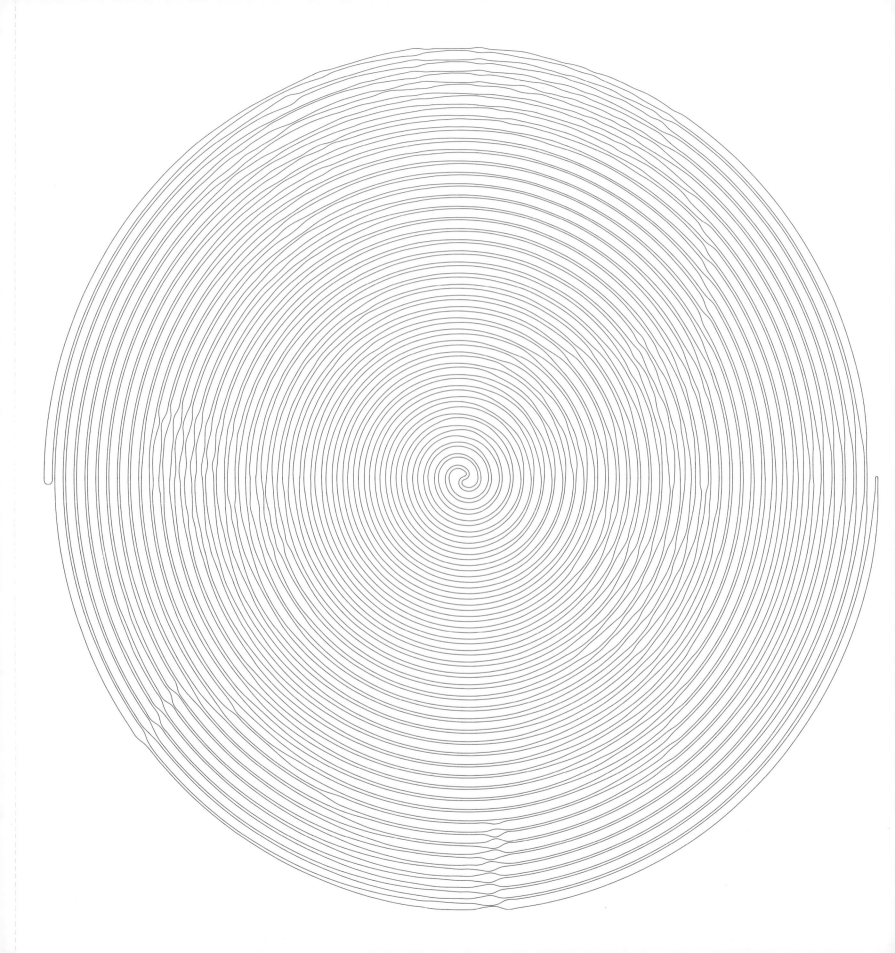

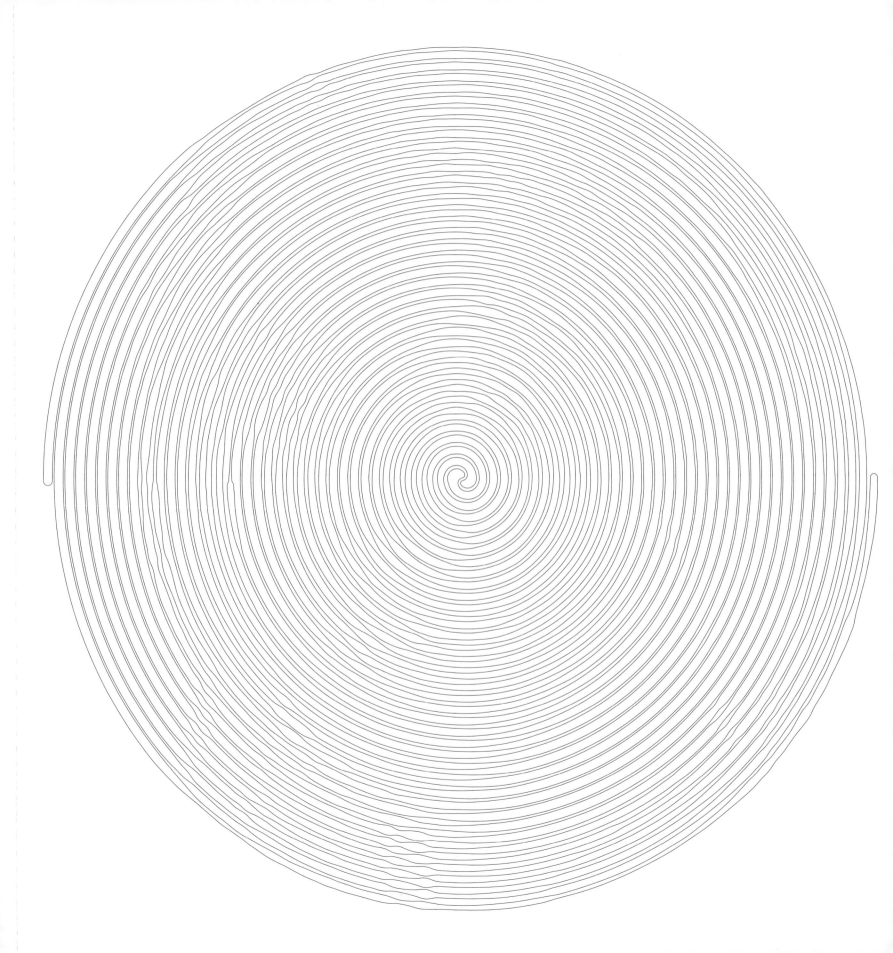

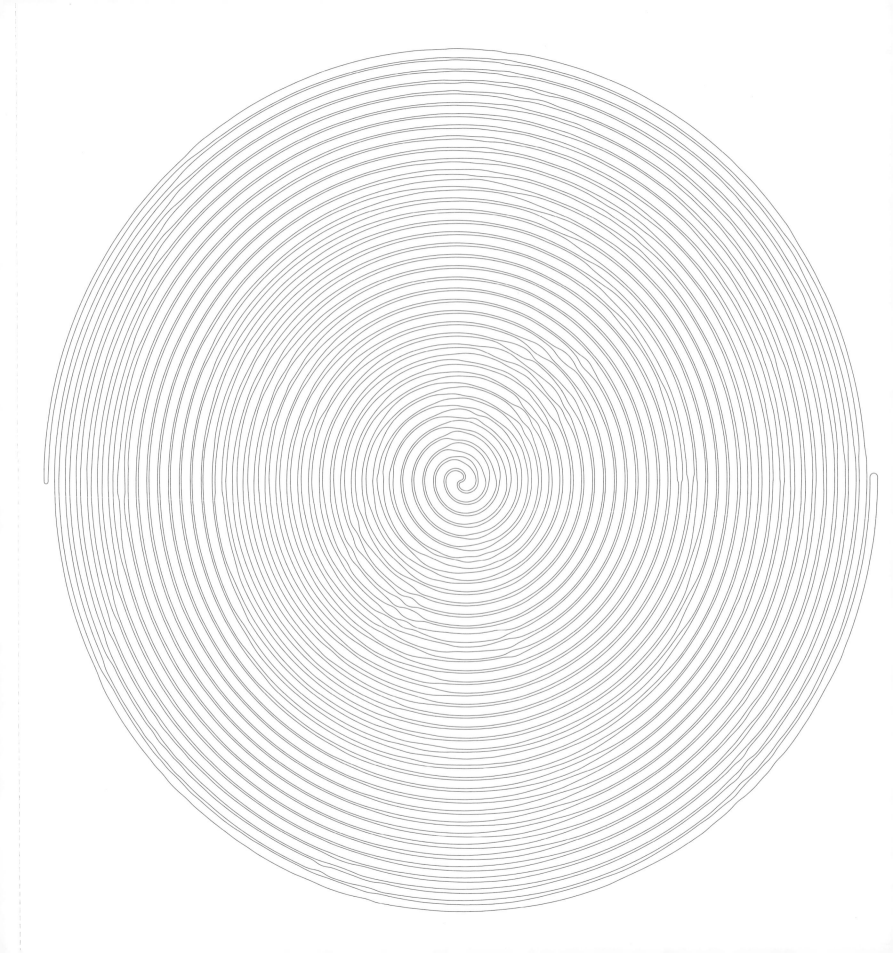

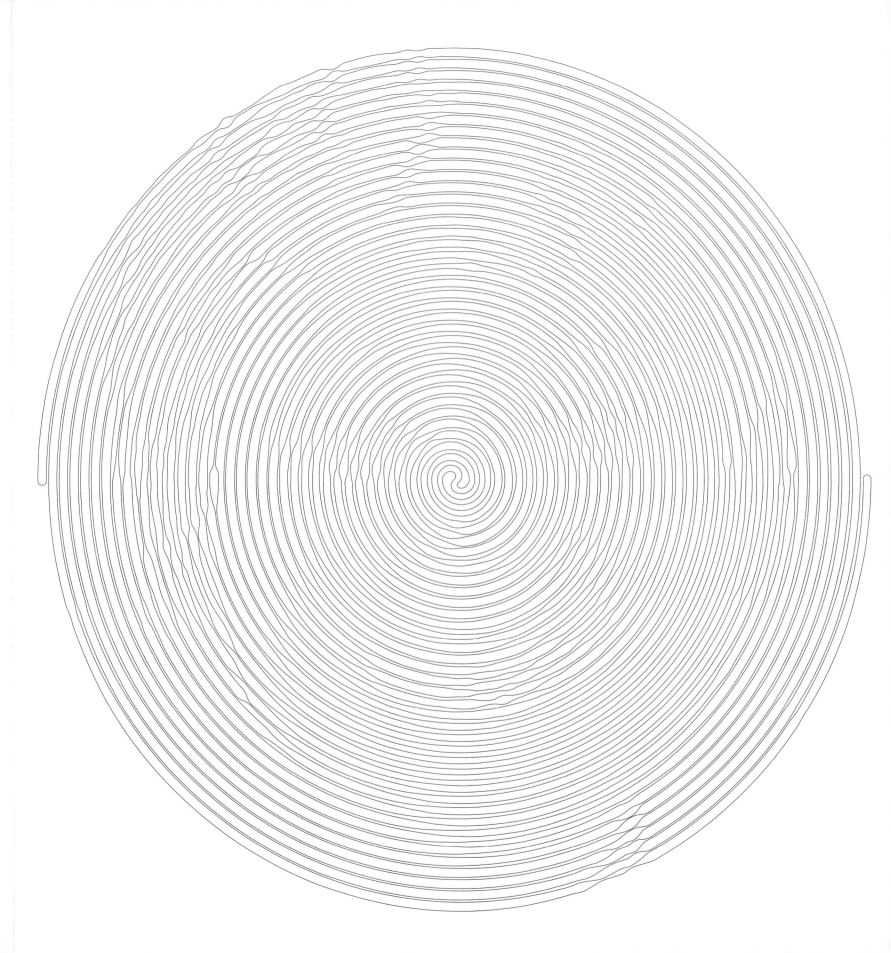

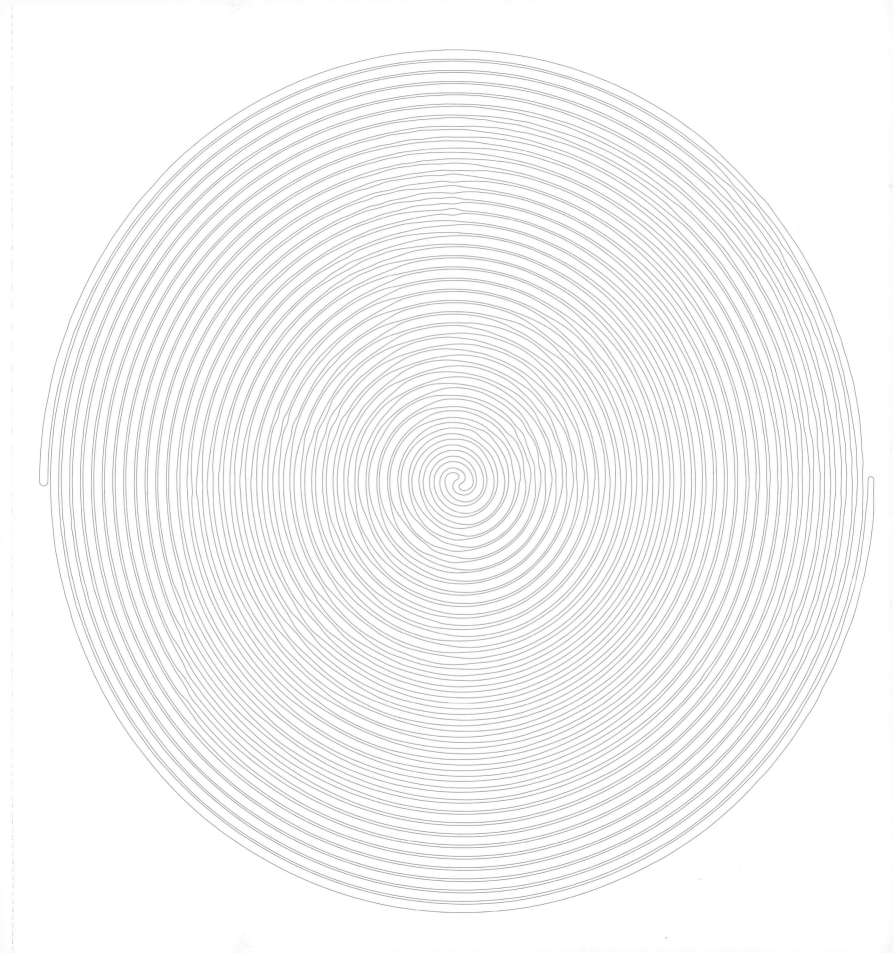

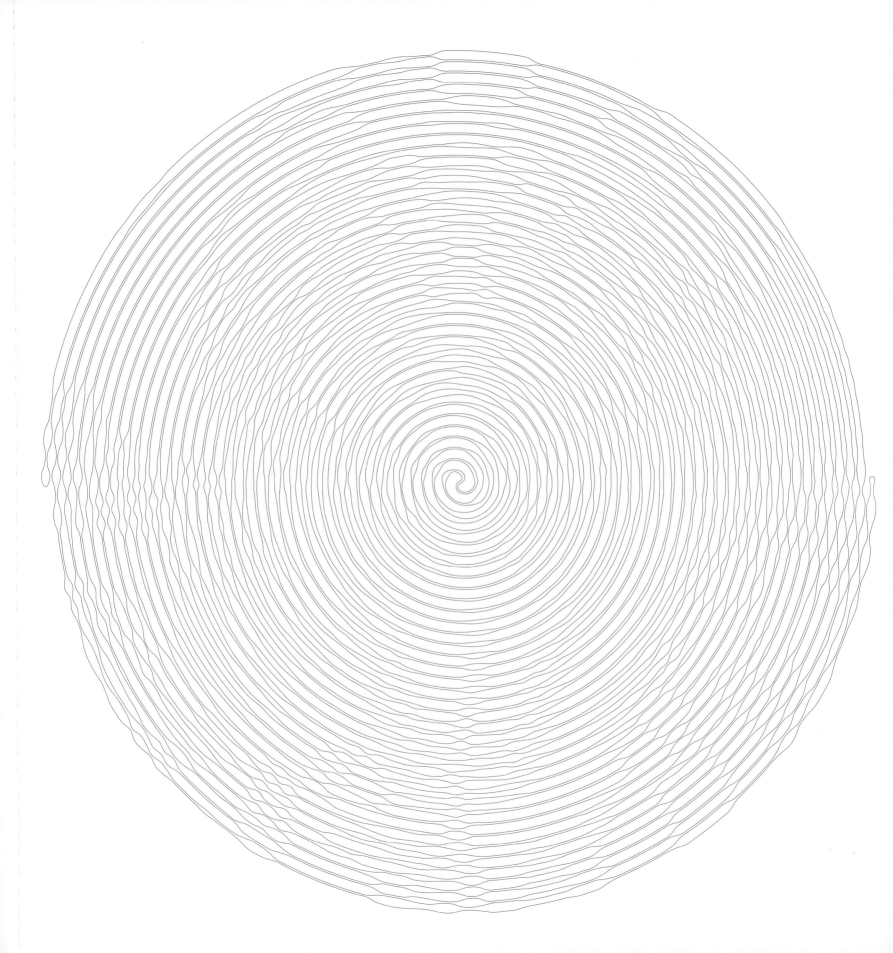

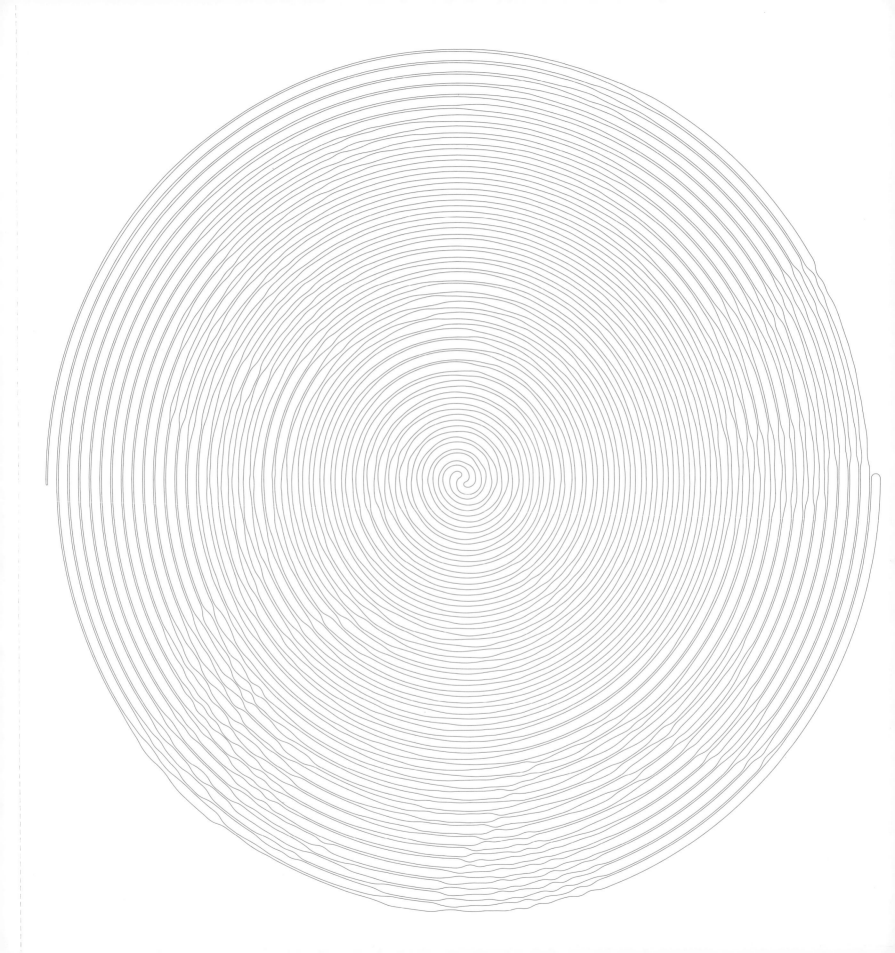